AF574094

# The Big Puddle

**Elspeth Graham**

**Illustrated by Ian Newsham**

OXFORD
UNIVERSITY PRESS

It rained and rained and rained.

The rain made a big puddle.

The puddle got bigger

and bigger

and bigger.

Poppy ran. She didn't look.

“Look out!” shouted Mr Tucker.

Poppy fell in the big puddle.

"Come with me," said Mrs Best.

Poppy was cold and wet.

Mrs Best looked in the box.

Now Poppy was warm and dry.

She was a bear!

It was time to go home.
Poppy ran to her dad.

Aaah!

"Come with me," said Mrs Best.